FIELD GUIDE
FOR
ACCIDENTS

NATIONAL POETRY SERIES

The National Poetry Series was established in 1978 to ensure the publication of five collections of poetry annually through five participating publishers. The Series has been funded over the years by Amazon Literary Partnership, the Gettinger Family Foundation, Bruce Gibney, HarperCollins Publishers, the Stephen and Tabitha King Foundation, Lannan Foundation, Newman's Own Foundation, Anna and Olafur Olafsson, Penguin Random House, the Poetry Foundation, Hawthornden Foundation, Elise and Steven Trulaske, and the National Poetry Series Board of Directors.

THE NATIONAL POETRY SERIES
WINNERS OF THE 2023 OPEN COMPETITION

Post-Volcanic Folk Tales by Mackenzie Schubert Poloyni Donnelly
Chosen by Ishion Hutchinson for Akashic Books

The Sky Was Once a Dark Blanket by Kinsale Drake
Chosen by Jacqueline Trimble for University of Georgia Press

Playing with the Jew by Ava Winter
Chosen by Sean Hill for Milkweed Editions

the space between men by Mia S. Willis
Chosen by Morgan Parker for Penguin

Field Guide for Accidents by Albert Abonado
Chosen by Mahogany L. Browne for Beacon Press

FIELD GUIDE
FOR
ACCIDENTS
POEMS

ALBERT ABONADO

WITH A **FOREWORD** BY **MAHOGANY L.** BROWNE

BEACON PRESS • BOSTON

BEACON PRESS
Boston, Massachusetts
www.beacon.org

Beacon Press books
are published under the auspices of
the Unitarian Universalist Association of Congregations.

© 2024 by Albert Abonado
Foreword © 2024 by Mahogany L. Browne

All rights reserved
Printed in the United States of America

27 26 25 24   8 7 6 5 4 3 2 1

This book is printed on acid-free paper that meets the uncoated paper
ANSI/NISO specifications for permanence as revised in 1992.

Text design and composition by Kim Arney

Library of Congress Cataloging-in-Publication Data

Names: Abonado, Albert, author. | Browne, Mahogany L., writer of foreword.
Title: Field guide for accidents : poems / Albert Abonado ;
with a foreword by Mahogany L. Browne.
Identifiers: LCCN 2024019312 (print) | LCCN 2024019313 (ebook) |
ISBN 9780807020517 (trade paperback) | ISBN 9780807020524 (ebook)
Subjects: LCGFT: Poetry.
Classification: LCC PS3601.B55 F54 2024 (print) | LCC PS3601.B55 (ebook) |
DDC 811/.6—dc23/eng/20240502
LC record available at https://lccn.loc.gov/2024019312
LC ebook record available at https://lccn.loc.gov/2024019313

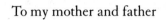
To my mother and father

CONTENTS

FOREWORD

Field Guide for Accidents begins with a prayer and carries us through nature among the wings of birdsong and a mother's healing psalms. Each poem betwixt breath and faith. Faith in God and faith in the loss of one's identity. The line breaks and the lemons illuminated. The insistence of a family silence and the temptation to follow the sound of one's internal weeping, all a joyous unearthing.

The text, both scientific in fact and devout in humanity, wields the power to expose the flesh of how death, God, and blueberries all have a song of their own. The author writes with a deft hand towards the knowing and the inarticulation of feeling, the practice of balance and bodies off-axis, oscillating between memory and rememory. This collection is a declaration. Small wolves, horses, trees, honeybees, rice, blessings, and ground beef. The specificity of living coaxes its audience through each section as dutifully as a theater's usher.

In the poem "The God I Know Eats with Its Hands," the author offers:

> I ask the god about the rules to mahjong, about the fires
> that burned a town but not a small wooden boy
>
> in a pine box. In a house full of gods,
> all the children are made of wood. Lord,

you curved stars into metatarsals, knotted
the cells behind my mother's breast before

the doctors harvested them, built a peach
from the sun.

The delicate handiwork of archiving a family's history without fear of dishonoring a bloodline. Each poem is a piece in the puzzle in the act of metamorphization or the humble art of praise or the study of ecopoetics or the undoing of our greatest worries.

In this collection, couplets turn into family photo albums and odes reverberate like fine-tuned pianos. The author is playing us a song, one that anyone can sing along to if there is a pulse beneath your skin. The author explores the restrictive nature of respectability while writing about intimacy—

My family insists such private
gestures do not belong
to an American public—
our hunger must be
as quiet as rice.

—and rediscovers racism in the fraught hands of friends:

*You showed your white friend that none of this bothered you,
that you knew how to ride alongside him, that you weren't
sensitive, not a whiny punkass, you knew how to take it, and
each time you laughed you widened your jaw, you showed him
your teeth, you dared him to look into your mouth to see the
metal bands straightening your jaw into an American smile.*

There isn't one way into this collection without exposing your own wounds. So lean in, reader. Loosen the necktie from your imagination's curve and watch Albert Abonado sculpt human from stone.

—MAHOGANY L. BROWNE
Italy, 2023

I

FROM THE TREES FULL OF BIRDSONG
COMES UNRIPE FRUIT

after Rick Barot

How I start a prayer: with the same hand I use
to lift food to my mouth, I draw a line down

to my navel pulling a zipper or curtain string
to reveal the small wolf in my belly, the one I feed

fat and vinegar. This is also how I pray: at eleven, I leapt
off the roof of my house. It was autumn

and everything that surrounded me collapsed
back into the dirt. I wanted to practice

my falling, feel the earth bend beneath my arrival, convinced
I would not break. When my mother prays

in her garden after the surgery on her arm and neck,
I listen to her bones grind beneath her skin.

She plants tulips, brushes a root from her hair, slices
for dinner that evening the garlic and onions she will sauté

in a wok with ground beef. And this, too, is a prayer,
my father rolling up his sleeve to reveal the long scar

on his arm to a room full of strangers at the garage
where they kept the wreckage of his car—a prayer

about the flesh around a knuckle and the alloys
the body will not reject. By prayer

I mean I read the same poem over and over,
until my hair becomes sloppy with poem, that I eat

it slowly until it coats my mouth. All my prayers begin
with hunger, a prayer in the shape of cold

fried chicken at my uncle's wake, in the blood stew I fail
to replicate. My wife wants to know why I reduce my poems

to something that fits in my mouth. I don't tell her I buried
my relatives in my throat, that my prayers belong to other
          voices.

When I pray, I can't hear my acid reflux gurgle, but the trees
full of birdsong, the tires hiss as they pass over a wet

road. This is a prayer full of rain and fog, weather soaked
          through
my old shoes, the thin fabric that contains the storm beneath
          my feet.

If by prayer we also mean the stories that we did not know
came before us, then this is also a prayer: my father stepping

away while they lowered his father into the ground
as we tossed white flowers onto his coffin, the hour

in which my brothers and I turned to one another and asked
where did he go, what is he doing now?

MANO

To the young boy who raises my wrist
to his forehead: I apologize
for the blessing I cannot provide—forgive
me for what my hands forgot: scales
on the piano, phone numbers of old
homes, the honeybee crawling through
my fingers before it stung me. I do not carry
around my years but shed them
like a husk. Your hands
may also betray you one day, linger
on a surface waiting for a memory
to flood your muscles. The hours
are a syrup you poured into your skin,
the sweetness behind your snap. I once
lifted my grandfather's wrist like this,
to my forehead after a stroke stripped him
of his English, after he whistled into
the evening while he plucked the hairs
from his chin. If I perform a gesture enough
times, it becomes a holy reflex. I pressed
his heat and weight into mine until the air
thickened to a silt between our palms.
Once, he held up to my face a bird he trapped.
Once, I held a bird for too long, it stopped singing.

SHE CARRIES MY LOLA INTO THE BATHROOM

If you must know, your lola weighs less
than a pigeon. I will not tell her

you are afraid to touch. How
do I know? I see your hands

shrink into your pockets. How do
you choose when to open your fingers?

You should know your skin
will grow tired like hers, one day.

Time is contagious.
She once complained

about my bony elbows,
about the way I squeezed

her ribs when I lifted her out
of her chair, said I folded her

like I delivered mail.
What was I trying to do?

God can wait, she said.
She still has

her chickens, the orchids,
the sound of rain

on the roof
of the chapel.

Don't forget to set me a plate
of rice for dinner when I die.

I don't want to forget
how to press the grains

against my palate.
Poked me so hard

in the chest when she spoke
I swear her fingers shattered.

Did you know she sings
the names of your mother

and her siblings in her sleep?
I didn't recognize them

the first time I lay beside her
for the night. Now,

they slide into my ear
like a rosary made

from sea glass while I inhale
the powder on her neck.

I know her better
than any parent did.

Do you think the dead
recognize one another, compare

notes on the lines inherited
from a history of faces?

Be honest. You believed
they plucked me out

of a tree, ripened to carry
your lola on my shoulders,

to listen to her bowel movements
shake the dry wall.

But what fruit has arms
like mine, recalls

dietary restrictions
with the same breath

it recites the Nicene Creed?
Why do I tell you this?

I want someone
to know what it means

to wait, to be polite
to the ghosts

in the kitchen, to turn this ring
on my finger while I listen

to her breath
pause in the dark.

ODE TO KAMAYAN

Because I want to taste
the lacquer of the coffee
table in which I scratched
an afternoon of names.
Because I want the elephant
I traced into the shoulder
of my wife to rest
under my tongue.
Because when I say
devotion, I mean any desire
I can squeeze in my palm
like a grapefruit.
With my fingers I press my rice
into a temple or gravestone,
depending on what my hunger
does that day, then scoop it
into my mouth, careful not to waste
one precious and delightful grain.
No, I can't explain the difference
between spoon and fingernail
except the distance and time
each takes to reach my mouth.
Why do I need a reason
for my joy, anyway?
My family insists such private
gestures do not belong
to an American public—
our hunger must be

as quiet as rice.
I watched my father
do the same after he returned
home in the morning,
his hands shaded by grease
after another overnight
shift in the subways
as my brothers and I purged
the sleep from our eyes.
Spam and eggs and rice.
The mound he gathered
under his thumb soaked
any oil or sauce or whatever
he spilled but wanted to save.
The van was stolen, he said
as his fingers burrowed
into his mouth like snakes.
How did you get home? asked my mother.
I reconstruct his face, the mole
on his left nostril illuminated
by fluorescent light, the eggs
that clung to his lips.
Every time I imagine my father's eyes
they disappear, but I can recall
the roach he smeared under his boot.
What was his answer?
It doesn't matter.
He pulled his glistening fingers
clean from his mouth.

THE GOD I KNOW EATS WITH ITS HANDS

When the god I know wears my skin, it stretches out
the sleeves for more room, eats chicken adobo

with its hands, drags a hunk of rice across
the plate to soak up the vinegar. The god I know

complains all the time about the shape
of my mouth, wants to know how I learned

to spell with a tongue like this. I apologize
to my god. I never imagined a mouth besides this one.

I ask the god about the rules to mahjong, about the fires
that burned a town but not a small wooden boy

in a pine box. In a house full of gods,
all the children are made of wood. Lord,

you curved stars into metatarsals, knotted
the cells behind my mother's breast before

the doctors harvested them, built a peach
from the sun. I have my own tricks, can make

my skin so transparent, my neighbors see
my heart glisten before I disappear. I can shrink

until I am no larger than a nail clipping, than the fibers
of a wool sweater, reduced to a single orange stripe.

Lord, I can teach you how to carry the volcanoes
your parents dreamed about, their fields of blueberries,

the men who stop you at night and ask you to recite
the pledge of allegiance. I can even cleave myself

in two. I will let you touch those seams. Lord,
let me show you how I float, how I levitate

small fruit when I am hungry and cannot
reach anything.

THE HISTORY OF PRAYER

When Drake sang *Oh my God, oh my God,*
if I die I'm a legend, I felt that—what prayer

doesn't start as half a racket
about memory, as a bell

in our gullet.
Every bruise is a hymn

that did not make its way back
to the heart. Lately,

I've been studying the role
iron contributes to our oxygen,

the amount that magnetizes blood.
The word hemoglobin unfolds

in my mouth like a paper frog.
Turns out, I'm already filled with rust.

What transfigures the blood into a thief?
I could try Catholicism again.

My family always arrived late
to Mass for reasons too numerous

to recall now, my shirt usually
tucked into my underwear.

We glowed in the shiny forehead
of the priest as he offered

this body, this blood,
said share this cup, this spit.

Everything I wish to save
dissolves under my tongue, a kiss

for the next person to retrieve
once we leave, once they've said Amen.

HOW TO REMOVE A SPIKE

Gratitude arrives with a hole in each hand, with metal
recycled from television sets and car fires.

This is the closest anyone has been
to my bones, shrapnel that makes its own music

as it passes through my body, a country
of volcanoes and sugar and kidney failure.

The nails are not enough to sustain me. Devotion
suspends but does not give permission to float.

The Health Department insists on tetanus shots,
that each spike be sterilized before it penetrates, blessings

pulled from a jar of liquor that also purifies.
This is how I was meant to be born: my hair made

from clouds the color of grease and the smoke
I carry everywhere. When they raise me

up, all the incense rises to my lips. I have the best
view of the sky, of the distance prayers

must travel and the dust they leave behind,
of the birds that swallow them on their way up.

TO PREPARE
THE BITTER MELON

You do not eat
what your father eats.

Too bitter,
you complain.

Your father knows
I am good

for the heart.
Ask anyone

who offers me a strip
of their tongue.

You will learn to love
my puckered skin.

I liberate
the blood.

Your family cultivated
me, but you

never learned to construct
a trellis high enough

for me to climb.
Would you believe me

if I said my root
system resembles

the head of your favorite
saint? I made

your dreams bloom
green, wrapped

your throat while
you slept, drifted

into the yards
of neighbors

who asked you
to explain my flavor:

Like a copper fingernail
Like a cloud of thumbtacks

Like a field of horses
that graze on your throat.

You tried the word
your father gave you,

you once dislocated your jaw
to refuse my entry:

Ampalaya,
repeated again

until my name
no longer squirmed

in your mouth,
and you could claim

I always belonged
to your body.
.

What do you know
about bitterness anyway?

Your family did not teach
you Tagalog, worried

other children did not
understand what

your desire means
in another language.

Every word you practice
fidgets for release

from your pinched lips.
The silence between you

and your mother prickles
your tongue.

I do not remember
the last time

you invited me
beyond your teeth.

You wait
until enough

distance separates
you and the knot

I made of your throat.
I will still be here.

You will learn
to love me, pair me

with onion and tomatoes
with ground pork and eggs

with vinegar and salt.
I, too, can be patient.

The mouth never
forgets.

RIVAL

My brother and I liked to play the game "I got your nose."
I would take his nose and he would take mine. Once, I lost
his nose and pretended this was a new phase of the game. He
kept asking for his nose, and I kept promising to return it.
Our relationship went on like this for years. When I found
his nose, he was already dead. I felt terrible because the nose
had nowhere to go. Now, I keep it in my shirt pocket next to
my birthstone as a tribute to my grief. I moisturize the nose.
Maintain its healthy pores. Salicylic acid wash. Activated
charcoal strips. Each night I read *The Collected Stories of Gogol*
to the nose. I hold it up to the light. We make shadow puppets.
Mostly birds. When we are both lonely, I stick a finger inside
the nose. I try to make it sneeze.

FOR ALL OF MY UNBORROWED AND UNSPENT JOYS

I play my favorite game where no one tells me I can't suck the
water from the hose on my lawn without thanking the white
people that came before me, that I need to be grateful for the
fish my parents pulled from the Long Island Sound, whose
heads they severed, whose jellied eyes they sucked, or I should
leave, go back to whatever place I call home. I replace their
word for lucky with the pineapple I ate after my grandfather's
funeral, with the moon over a river full of my aunts and
cousins, with the first time I folded lumpia that did not
separate in the oil, with the water I sugared with Kool-Aid or
Tang or anything that leaves my tongue feeling gritty, with
the sun grown too hot I draw the shades, sit in my underwear
and let the fan blow across the elastic of my boxers, with the
joy of a fried egg sandwich, the yolk spilling down my chin
when I ask my wife if she would like to lick my neck and she
does this slowly, or the joy of two radio stations whose signals
overlap while driving to my parents. What a joy to know both
songs and not have to choose, to sing both at once. O, I am
ready to die from all that joy, to sliver that joy from marrow
to cochlea, my throat a ditch dug from this joy, joy for the acid
and sweetness of our bellies and joy for the text I sent to my
brother asking if he's okay and he responded yeah and that
was enough.

II

If this statement is true, then Caril obviously believed at the time that her stepfather was still alive, for her to have on the spot concocted a lie that would serve to demonstrate that she believed her family was still alive would require an incredibly quick and clever mind.

Does her testimony have the ring of truth? As discussed earlier, this highly subjective standard plays ominously or otherwise into many if not most credibility judgments, including that Caril's statement sounds like the truth. I also weigh it against the credibility of the maker of the only other version, Charlie Starkweather. If true, his version would show Caril to be not only mendacious but an out-and-out monster. She would have watched him kill her stepfather, shoot and smash her mother's head with a rifle butt until she fell on the floor, smash her baby sister's skull twice with the rifle butt, and whip a hunting knife into her throat to stop her crying. She would then sit and watch TV while he wrapped up and re-moved the three bodies and stuffed them in outbuildings, and afterward cleaned up the blood in the house. And then the two of them would have hung around the murder house for six days watching TV, having sex, and drinking pop and eating potato chips while her family lay bundled up and mixed outside only yards away. Nothing supports such a psychopathic personality; indeed, the facts show that Caril dearly loved her mother and cherished her baby sister. No facts other than those offered by Charlie in later statements indicate a cicebeartatness sufficient to cause her, after witnessing her family's bloody execution, to turn to their killer and ask calmly, "What do we do now?" and settle in to watch TV.

Perhaps Caril was a multiple personality, the quiet, kind Caril who loved children and wanted to be a nurse versus the stone-cold Caril who killed innocents without remorse. However, by definition, a multiple personality switches back and forth between the various personalities as circumstances change, and Caril was only the killer Caril all the time for eight days. One could always argue that for some reason the store in the personality of the kind, child-loving Caril and never switched back to the killer.

All of this must be weighed against the evidence showing that Caril in fact knew her parents were dead, most of which consisted of statements

PUNCHLINE

Your white friend let you know that it's okay for him to make jokes about Black people as long as he joked about white people too. This is a democracy, after all, he promised. See how whiteness uses whiteness to justify itself. Your parents sent you to a high school full of white boys like him where you learned how to be friends with them, how to share your Doritos with them on the bus, how to dislike the smell of dried fish and soy sauce. What else does he have to offer?

He told another joke, this time about Mexicans, about Indians, about the Polish, about Italians and blonde women. You were on the late bus returning home or the backseat of his car while his father drove. You showed your white friend that none of this bothered you, that you knew how to ride alongside him, that you weren't sensitive, not a whiny punkass, you knew how to take it, and each time you laughed you widened your jaw, you showed him your teeth, you dared him to look into your mouth to see the metal bands straightening your jaw into an American smile, yes, you gestured by tipping your chin up. You have always had other ways of surviving with your mouth that doesn't involve eating.

Your white friend didn't stop there—he joked about the Chinese too. Do you get it? You are not Chinese—you are Pinoy—so you say you do. Of course. Obviously, you get *it*. Your white friend didn't know about the Philippines and you didn't tell your white friend the jokes you knew, the ones about the money lost at cockfights, about lateness, about the blood your relatives see as nurses, as caretakers of wealthy children, not the ones about the money they send back to their provinces, not the dogs that your family would supposedly eat.

Your father joked he once ate dog and washed it down with San Miguel. This was how you pictured him: at a card table with a spread of dog kaldereta and dog adobo and dog lumpia, a bowl of rice and banana leaves, the clatter of mahjong tiles sliding around on a table you don't see, smoke from the fire over which they roasted a dog mixed with the cigarettes your father tried to quit. No, you didn't tell your white friend this story about the father you dreamt about, scooping dog into his mouth, your father as a young man with his original teeth.

Each visit to your father reveals a new line on his face around his lips or eyes, lines that deepen over time, your father who sleeps in the reclining chair to the sirens of the game show *The Chase* that clot the living room—a plate of rice and chicken bones and mango skins rests on the coffee table in front of him. Your white friend doesn't know your father like this, your father who covers his mouth after removing his teeth for the evening, your father interrogated by police officers at night while he adjusted the attachments to the sprayer, his tractor starlit, parked along the road, your father who checked the tank for leaks, who drenched the air with malathion.

The officers pulled over to ask your father why he worked so late at night, the officers who didn't know about the overnight shifts he worked for the MTA until retirement, the officers didn't travel with your father to Chinatown on Saturday mornings, your father who told them this is my farm, told them I live here, have lived here since I retired, your father who said this is what I wanted: to care for these bushes, to protect the bees; your father who chose this sun, these hills, your father with dirt under his fingernails, the dirt of glaciers and volcanoes, your father at the Knights of Columbus, your father who donates to the sheriffs' association. The officers who wanted your father's identification said they heard reports of a gunshot, and how does your father answer for that? You imagine the kinds of guns that thrived in their heads. *Gunshot?* you say. *Out here, someone is always firing a gun.*

REMEDY

Either my father makes the sign of the cross on my wrist

with ginger or he uses garlic. One of these cures fever.

One of these is not Catholic. I can't decide. I close

my eyes. I taste the garlic again, the ginger,

the heat of my father's fingers in my mouth.

I picture him holding my wrist—And in his other hand?

Not garlic, but a tooth. Where does a father

take all the teeth he loses? He leaves one in my pocket.

I press the tooth into my chest, make it into a new heart.

None of this is true. I start over. This time with ginger.

This time I am in bed. I can see the squirrel by the window

with the bread it retrieved from our trash. I call to the squirrel

but remind myself this part is also a lie I use to find

my father: the squirrel, the bed, the angry forehead

my father presses with the back of his hand.

I tell him slow down. I want to smell the soil

under his fingernails. I can't see my father's face

when he prays. That, too, erodes. I replace his face

with more hair, with chicken feed and leather, with salt water

and goat eye. He holds my hand this time

with my palms faced up as if I am about to catch rain.

He squeezes around the wrist. It hurts until I remind myself

there are no nerves in my memories. I must have seen

him do something like this before. Not the bedroom

but the kitchen, maybe, or the backyard with its crabapples

and sparrows, with the bitter melons climbing

into our neighbor's yard. I need

to start again and admit this is all wrong:

my father, the ginger, the smell of vinegar. No,

in the beginning, my father was a root

I extracted and carved over and over

until I recognized his face.

WITNESS

Witness my father who drives and hums the notes to a song I do not recognize. I

do not ask him to clarify, worried he would stop

and diminish the magic of his throat as we travel along

the Susquehanna. Witness the clouds that resemble a hive

of bees, the crows and the triumph of their carrion, the river that could carry

our faces if we came close enough. Witness that my favorite color

is blue for reasons that remain unclear—say blue is the color of forgiveness,

the color of vowels and my father's snoring.

In the distance between our seats, his head shrinks. If I study

my father long enough, he may fit across

a knuckle. Some afternoons, when I was younger, he rested his head

in my lap so I could extract his white hairs. *Itchy* he complained—

about their stiffness, about time. I am roughly the same age

he was when he would ask me to cradle his head away from my sticky

brothers, my fingers nimbler then. *At this rate, you won't have any*

hair left, my brothers and I would tell him, but in that silence, he slept

while I tested the tenderness of his scalp, worried I might pull

the wrong thread and unravel my father, forced to spool his head together—

what child does not worry about reassembling their parents

when asked?   What would I have told my mother then? I pulled

and pulled on my father, wondering how this will end.

YOU ARE SUPPOSED TO CUT A MANGO INTO SQUARES

All this talk   about writing   from the diaspora

How to be a mango   Be still and silent

My mother never hesitates   with her knife

slices around the pit   *This was my uncle's favorite part*

she says softly   as if he would disapprove

of her gossip   *He would leave most*

of the fruit for himself   I picture myself inside

the smoke and rice of her story   somewhere at her table

between knife and skin and seed   my uncle's face covered

in nectar   How could anyone eat this and remain clean?

Who trusts a mouth   that does not abandon itself

to this ripeness?   I pull from my teeth

the fibers of a meal   I do not remember

What are you doing   with your fingers? asks my wife

No one was supposed to know

OUTER BANKS

I have a poem that starts like this: my mother
came back as a haunted boat. I spend
most of the poem trying to decide
if I should escape the boat, if I should forgive
my mother, or if I am the one who needs
to be forgiven. The poem ends
when the boat sinks, becomes a new reef.
It ends when I visit my haunted boat mother
to catalog the eels and crabs, the mollusks
under the hull. I even swim with the sharks
and feed them shrimp. I put this poem away,
call my mother on her birthday. I don't tell her
about the haunted boat in my poem or the slow flood
that overwhelmed her. I don't tell her where
the boat sank. It needed to be someplace I could still reach,
where I could practice holding my breath,
where the light could penetrate glass underwater.
Anyway, it is her birthday and she tells me
I should donate her body to science
when she dies, whisked away to a room
where science can do what science does
with the dead, until they reduce her to ash, which is
the economical thing to do. All she wants,
she says, is a light dinner, maybe a few
prayers said in her memory. We could talk
about her recipes, but I have more questions
like, what about a resurrection
and how does a poem come to this?

RECOLLECTION

What did they feed you on the flight?

      What were your options? Do you remember

what it was like to eat above your parents

      for the first time? What did you take

with you? What did you leave behind?

      Did you brush your teeth? Did you remove

your shoes during the flight? Do you remember

      the kind of plane you rode? Did it look

like a tongue? What was the color

      of the carpet and how did it feel

under your toes? How dark

      does the ocean get at night?

Did you dream

               about your children in America?

Did you know

about the birthmark on my nose?

How sharp did you imagine

the teeth of my brothers would be?

What was the name of the movie you watched? How long

was your hair? What kind of music

did they play? Do clouds sing hymns

at a certain elevation? Did you recite

the Hail Mary when the plane ascended?

Did you recognize the sun as your own

in this country? When you called your mother,

did she recognize your voice? What did you spend

to get here? What did you need

when you arrived? What did you want

to forget?

INSTEAD OF THE MASTECTOMY

We talked about
the reclaimed

tulip bulbs gone
rotten over winter.

We could not
save them all,

irredeemable,
waiting

for the soil
to turn yellow.

We don't use
the word loss

in this house.
The seasons

still change
without us.

There was nothing
left to do.

YOU MUST WAIT 15 MINUTES BEFORE YOU TRY AGAIN

Your mother in her hospital bed asks you to remember

her password for   No that is wrong   She retraces

the history of her password back to her own mother

to her favorite verse in Genesis   Try again   you say

Here is a captcha   Which upright horse belongs to your
    mother?

Separate the teeth from the stars

You have permission to fail   three times and then

you must wait   How to decode

your mother   How to be patient   Start

with the namelessness of your lola   You type oops

How to decode your mother   Invert her   No

What is the opposite of bloodline?   Delete

the stars and start again: This time   a friend presents

pictures of her latest fetus   Oh you say   and wow

Already you imagine a glorious hairline a birthmark like Paris

and the size a head must reach before a face is a face

AN HONEST MISTAKE

My cousin holds his arm besides mine,

says my skin is not his skin.

My uncle asks do people know

you are Filipino? Haha I say.

Haha it must be the dimmer American sun.

Haha it must be the salt in the Atlantic.

Maybe I should drink from a different ocean.

America at the airport asks

for the name of my tribe, compliments me

for the Vietnam in the poems

another man read.

An honest mistake. Haha.

This is the burden of my America.

To transform.

To become invisible.

America does not acknowledge this.

They need more proof besides my imagination.

Where is my paperwork?

Not enough empirical evidence.

Forensics.

Think *CSI: Miami*.

David Caruso was special.

The glare of America was too much for David Caruso.

An America saturated with color.

Don't blame America when it forgets

what it leaves behind.

Blame the Scientific Method.

Blame my secret identity.

My secret identity is a crater on the moon.

You can only find me at night.

A *Wall Street Journal* headline asks "Too Many Asians?"

They already corrected the headline.

An honest mistake.

This is their secret identity.

My mother traces the bridge

of my nose, says it's not broad

like hers or my father, wonders why

it grew so crooked, asks

when did it break and how do you

breathe when you sleep?

FIELD GUIDE FOR ACCIDENTS

To save a ticket for a future ride, to prevent the LIRR conductors from collecting ours, we high school boys slept, listened carefully for the doors that rattled open as people traveled from one car to the next. We knew how to watch for the conductors, whose steps came accompanied by something jingling from their belts: keys, change. We knew better than to sit close to one another, so we scattered throughout the train. On a good day, the conductor passed us, left us to our lies. There were days the conductors were not so charitable and shook us awake. We were committed though, fluttering our eyes as we opened them, as if we needed to adjust to the light around their faces, confused someone had the authority to release us from our dreams.

How I pretended to sleep: I imagined traveling into the dark branches of my lungs to fill them with air, made every breath a heavy strain on my chest. I gave my body to gravity. My sleep is substantial. My sleep has weight. I make myself immovable, difficult to lift. I pretended to sleep so that I did not have to pay. I pretended to sleep so my father would carry me from the car to the bed. Sometimes, this was not a lie, and I succumbed to a rest I didn't know I needed, woke up disoriented by my own performance.

I was in fourth grade when, after school, I played Jerome, the Polynesian son of Emile, for a dinner theater performance

of *South Pacific*. My father would wait in the car, where I
sometimes napped before the show. Once, I forgot to spit out
my gum before I slept and woke up to a wad of sticky hair.
Members of the cast tried to remove the gum with remedies
that included oils and peanut butter. Eventually, they had no
choice but to shave a small bald spot on my head. I learned
then that I couldn't trust my mouth while I slept.

My wife showed me a video she recorded of me snoring on her
hip because I didn't believe those sounds belonged to me.

From my bed, I watch my neighbor's motion lights flicker.
What animals pass beyond my periphery: opossum, raccoon,
crow? I listen for the syncopation of black walnuts that
fall from the trees above my car and provoke my car alarm
through the evening. I've ignored the sirens before and
discovered too late the busted window. I've run into the lot
barefoot at night, hoping to disrupt a stranger. What did I
expect to find out there besides more darkness?

Symptoms of Sleep Deprivation:

1. *Memory:* You may forget your wallet. You may forget how
   to play your favorite song on the piano. You may forget the
   faces of your teachers as they hovered above you, guiding
   your cursive or correcting the notes of your sonata. You
   may forget the password to your mother's computer. You
   may forget the names of your relatives, of the people who

pray around your parents, the ones who insist you have met before. You may lie: Oh yes, I remember you. Thank you for coming. It's been too long.

2. *Mood Changes:* You may become more irritable. You may not want to commit to any projects. You may always answer: Maybe later. You may want to stare out the window, scroll through the selections on Netflix or Amazon Prime. You may try to call your mother, who repeats the same sentence about her neck. You may regret calling in the first place.

3. *Weakened Immunity:* You may experience nasal drip. You may search WebMD to determine the source of your headaches, your twitching eye. This will be a terrible idea. You will lose hours of sleep recalling the videos of operations you observed, the cysts that burst, and lie in bed cataloging the surgeries your parents did not tell you about until after they were done.

4. *Concentration:* You may struggle to focus on the mouth of the person speaking to you. You may not understand what the words accident, father, mother mean when strung together in a sentence until you are in the hospital sitting bedside. You find objects in the room to focus your attention: the signs to the bathroom, the tube that snakes from your father's throat, the cotton swabs they use to moisten your mother's lips.

5. *High Blood Pressure:* You may forget your heart, so you press your finger against your wrist. You may have been told your arteries are strong, a good pulse. You may think blood and grief are the same word, may want to forget the

blood streaked across the airbags, pretend they belonged to another animal, believe your parents never bled.

6. *Poor Balance:* You may fall and fall again.

The recommended amount of sleep is 7.1 hours. The missing hours of sleep accumulate into a sleep deficit. How does one account for those missing hours? Categories for a spreadsheet for my family: these are the hours you lost for the uncle whose funeral you could not attend, these are the hours you lost to the revelations of cancer, of brain injury, my brother falling from a balcony, the hours you spent counting your debts, the unpaid heating bills, the phone bills, the hours late at night you called to see how your mother was doing, the minutes you spent promising to return soon, asking if she was comfortable, about her oxygen levels, hours you spent on the prayers for her safety.

- A Black person averages 6.05 hours of sleep.
- A Chinese person averages 6.35 hours of sleep.
- A Hispanic/Latinx person averages 6.56 hours of sleep.
- A white person averages 6.85 hours of sleep.
- The percentage of Black people who reported poor sleep quality is 8.3%.
- The percentage of Hispanic/Latinx people who reported poor sleep quality is 6.7%.
- The percentage of Chinese people who reported poor sleep quality is 6.6%.
- The percentage of white people who reported poor sleep quality is 5%.

The numbers confirmed what we already knew: white people sleep better and longer in America.

The Asian participants for this study were predominantly Chinese. I want to avoid substituting Chinese for Filipinx, but the temptation is hard to ignore. People have done this to me before, assumed I was Chinese, yelled a string of nonsense at me as I rode by on my bicycle. I want to be able to see my family in these studies. I want to imagine my parents with a festival of wires stuck to their foreheads and cheeks as they slept and the kind of questions they would have to answer. I want to know that their sleep habits are also worth scrutinizing, that there is more meaning to the time they do not set aside for themselves.

Saturday mornings, my brother and I would sometimes go with our father to Chinatown. We fell asleep waiting for him to return from the crowded streets, collecting merchandise for our store Pearl of the Orient, a Filipinx grocery located in a strip mall in Levittown, New York. Officers came to our window with questions about my father's double parking. We told the officers the same story each time: we didn't know where our father went but promised that our stay was only temporary.

With his head cradled in my lap, I pulled the white hairs from my father's scalp until he fell asleep. As my fingers parted his hair, touched the tender spots where the hair breaks the skin, his head became a country whose borders I never understood.

My father worked overnight shifts at the MTA and came home around the time my brothers and I were getting ready to leave for school. He would often be asleep when we returned. We tiptoed around the house, played games with our hands over our mouths, careful not to provoke him should he chase us with belt in hand, punish us for the time he could not get back.

The children of immigrants are supposed to sleep better than their parents. I assume this means we inherit the hours our parents have lost.

No, this isn't true. A country doesn't return the hours it takes from us.

Increased rates of fatal car accidents, heart attacks, and workplace injuries have all been attributed to daylight saving time.

The phrase spring forward sounds polite, even optimistic, progressive, but once we leap, where do we plant our feet?

My father sat on the edge of his bed, his back to me. He didn't see me studying him through the crack in his bedroom door. He was supposed to be getting ready for another overnight shift, but instead, he sat slouched and motionless. Maybe he was still dreaming. I waited for him to move, didn't leave until I could see his shoulders rise and fall as he took a breath.

What did I know, what did I know
Of love's austere and lonely offices?

I imagine my mother asleep on her flight from the Philippines to New York after accepting her first job in America. My grandparents didn't approve of her choice; they wanted her to be a teacher at the nearby school. Perhaps my mother dreamt about the children she left behind, a classroom of unopened books, or of her parents complaining about the clothes she didn't take with her. Perhaps my mother didn't dream at all, stretched out in the empty row, her shoes under her seat. Perhaps she had a mouth full of reheated chicken à la king as she stared out the window.

Perhaps it was daytime as she peered into the ocean, searching for the outlines of whales. Perhaps it was too dark for any of that, and she could only see the ghost of her face in the glass lit by the faint lights of wings, with no way to measure how far she had come, only the hum of the engines to tell her she still had further to go.

On long trips, my mother frequently pulled over to rest, steal a quick nap. We parked in the shoulder lane, in the empty driveway of a farm, at the rest stops, on the gore, that narrow triangle by the offramp where an officer once came to our window to check if we were okay. My mother assured him we were fine, just sleepy, but he insisted we couldn't stay, it wasn't safe. He made her choose: take the exit or keep going.

Tips for Alert Driving

1. *Adequate sleep offers the best protection.* Do not stay up late to check your phone for any messages about your parents' accident. Do not research the survival rate of car accidents. Do not compare age groups. Do not watch videos about brain injury, spinal injury, about the amputation of limbs. Do not text your brother to see if he is up. He will not be. Do not remember all the moments their eyelids grew heavy. Do not promise that next time, you will be the one to drive.

2. *Avoid medication that might lead to drowsiness.* Know the names of the medication and the dosages your parents take, so when the hospital asks, you are not confused or uncertain about the answers to their questions. You do not say blood pressure when you mean cholesterol. You do not say aspirin when you mean insulin. Know, too, the name of the primary care physician, the one who moved to North Carolina. Know that they had been looking for a new physician, waiting for the doctor to provide recommendations. Know that, eventually, you will be responsible for this information too.

3. *Be vigilant.* Recognize the signals from your body that indicate you are tired, such as the sharp bob of your head or the drift into the rumble strip. Recognize the muscles that can no longer support your neck, the erratic twitch that leads you to press the heel of your palm against your eyes until everything goes black. Recognize the difference between anticipating what you will find in the hospital

based on the photographs your cousins texted you and the dream you had while driving, the one of your father walking to the hospital window to complain about the gray weather.

4. *Caffeine is not enough.*

Note: You may still experience a brief loss of consciousness if you are seriously sleep-deprived, even after a cup of coffee. Consider a nap if you are drowsy.

Note: The relief these steps provide is temporary. You may have a long trip ahead for which you are not adequately prepared.

I rummaged through the wreckage to retrieve their missing luggage, their tablet, their fishing gear. Both of my parents slept as this car drifted into the woods. I pictured their weightless bodies as the car ricocheted from one tree to the next, their eyes closed, the cloud of dirt that trailed the car as it traveled from shoulder lane to grass. They didn't notice their limbs flail and collide with the dashboard, with the seat, with their sleeping faces, didn't notice the contents of my mother's purse scattered into the air around them to float among the slivers of glass, the clams they dug up from the beach, the sandals my mother slipped off her feet so she could stretch her toes. Each imagined reconstruction of this event ended the same. They remained untouchable. When I spoke with the owners of the garage where the car was kept, they told me about the ambulances and helicopters summoned to the scene, sirens neither parent heard.

On the way back from the Buffalo Valley Produce Auction, my father slept in the passenger seat. We had done this drive several times this summer. The route took us along the Susquehanna, passing through the verdant valleys of Pennsylvania, by fields of corn and tobacco, by the World of Little League Museum in Williamsport. After their accident, I did most of the driving, my father acting as guide, the one who collected the checks or negotiated with buyers. I knew my father as someone whose intense snores were inescapable—they regularly shred the air inside our house— but there in the van, I didn't notice him fall asleep. Looking over, I saw a portrait of my father sliding into another world. I remembered how easily his face could be broken. If I could have reached him then, bridged the gap between us, I might have squeezed his arm, nudged him, disturbed him until his eyes snapped open. I would have checked to make sure he'd wake up.

THE BEARS NEVER TALK ABOUT WINTER

You don't see the bears, but know they are there. How could they not be? America has so much to offer. Honey and blueberries. Overripe squash. Rabbits! According to your neighbors, they come for teriyaki sauce. They do not knock before they pry open the refrigerator door or push their faces into the cabinets, looking for something sweet. After, ants or flies come to clean their delicate faces while they sleep. Someone came with pictures of bear shit they found in a patch of milkweed. Your mother nodded, said yes, obviously, that is evidence that something did not leave our fields hungry, that you must be prepared to diagnose any encounter. Know the difference between the brown or black bear before you cover your neck or retrace your steps. This is how you play dead: Fold your arms across your chest. Conceal your pupils. Death is a performance. Make space for the other ghosts. Repeat the last question your grandmother asked: "Why do those children laugh?" You may be tempted to nap while you wait for the danger to pass, but you cannot. This is not the right time. You are about to become a remarkable story.

FLOOD WARNING

Say your car tips into a river, the river floods your throat. Say silt. Say cyanobacteria blooms on your tongue. Say the river is history or empathy. Say the river is a trail of condolences you did not send. Say the floods you know: Gilgamesh. Genesis. What animals did they take close to their chests? So much of our survival glistens in our memory. Say the name of a city you would like to visit drifts along the current. Most names rise to the surface. This is how you escape. Your mother told you about the aunt who did not follow her name, so she became a flood, her name swallowed by schools of catfish and dragged into the deep. The nature of the world is to consume you. You cannot trust it. It will not let you forget.

EVERY WILDERNESS IS A PROVINCE OF TEETH

The snakebite is never just a snakebite. The snake could be the borders of America or the lost history of peaches. What facts do you find instructive? The vestigial joints of their missing limbs the origin of sin. You should not withdraw venom with your lips, should not complain why the blood is not sweeter. Every good mouth knows when to be unhinged. Every hollow tooth conceals a promise. Never reach for an irritated snake, but, if you must, control the jawbone. Make it speak for you. Make it spell your grief. It can say the prayers you forgot, answer questions about your family tree. Soon, you replace your mouth with snake. Look how wide your mouth can grow, how you regurgitate bones. The snakes multiply. You cannot tell the difference between the snakes that are alive and the snakes that are dead. You worry about feeding them. Try bone soup, you say. Isn't this great? You will never be alone.

A COLONY OF ANTS ATTACK MY WRIST AND I JUST LET THEM

Because I am babysmooth and their teeth is a parade because they want to praise the labor of one another and because they tongue the smallest hairs to find honey and because I do not tell them that what they feed their children is mostly terror and sin because I want other marks besides ones that suggest my collection of failures because I believe in the hickey and any bruise that comes from the lips because I respect the size of any hunger because I can be terrifying and generous and offer blood to the small and the living because I am also a cathedral with glass instead of skin where everyone sees who prays and who sleeps because the sermon could have been punchier or used more sugar but everyone knows the priest means well and makes great coffee and pastries and once adopted a really sick dog, which he lets everyone pet, which we can all agree is something worth saving.

WOLF HOUSE

To survive the story, you identify eye, ear, fang. The order does not matter. A long nose hair dangles like a spider thread. *Lola*, you ask, *how often do you groom?* This is a wolf dressed for love and wine. The wolf with a velvet tongue. The tongue strokes your birthmarks. You must reconcile with this desire as it consumes you. *What a big mouth you have.* Your lola comes from a different darkness, admonishes you from within the hollow of the wolf body: *How could you not tell us apart?* Time diminishes all of us, Lola. Easier to disappear into the mouth. *Which way is out?* To live, we slice open our bellies. You already forget who among us was the wolf. When we are reborn, we must be ready to account for what we lost. A man who twists the handle of his ax stands over us and asks *How did you get here?* The wrong question. We were born like this. Our stomachs full of stones.

LANDSCAPE WITH CAR WRECK AND FATHER

The photograph is the dream. My father with jacket unzipped.
I recall a light rain. I want to describe the rain in my mouth,
but the rain is not part of this record. Over his shoulder: the
trees on the hills mostly stripped of their leaves, telephone wires.
Safe to assume that both of us had been breathing at the time.
A green field in one corner. The green spills everywhere. The
memory is not green. The study of my father will not change
this. I acknowledge the chassis, but I am not ready to discuss it.
Where to start. I draw a line from my father to the trees. A line
from the trees to the car. There must be a meaning to all of this.
A sense of purpose. For the tree. For the windshield. For the
scar hidden in his sleeve like a centipede. Meaning, meaning
everywhere. Not pictured: his feet, deflated airbag. Not pictured:
blood on the dashboard, men in a garage. I cannot draw a line
to what I cannot see. The photograph makes my father appear
further away. I measure his head against my thumb. How do
I approach him from this distance? I squish his face below my
thumb. He walks away from the wreck. Or towards the edge
of the frame. What difference does that make? I am the one on
the other side.

THE TREES ARE MOTHERFUCKERS

after Alan Dugan

I said what I said.
I don't trust
their patience during
long periods of thirst,
followed by colors
impossibly pulled up
from the dirt and light.
What is alive anyway?
I, too, know how to be
resentful and still
appear bright.
The television in the next
room fills the holes
of my face with enough
heat to cook an egg.
I make small wagers
on the little griefs
that occupy the screen.
I go to the woods
where I find nothing but names
I would never give
to my children.

SUMMER SOLSTICE WITH MOTOWNPHILLY AS SOUNDTRACK

For no reason in particular except that today is Tuesday and sunny and maybe because I haven't spoken to anyone in my family except to like a handful of pictures on Facebook. Who knows why we listen carefully for certain voices? I try to summon my grandfather's voice while next door my neighbor tears holes into the ground for whatever the reason. Neither I nor my grandfather can ignore the machinery working against my memory, my grandfather who opens his mouth to speak and instead we hear the churn of the backhoe's diesel engine, the collision of two heavy metal objects. He tries again and this time my neighbor's dirt comes tumbling out of his mouth. What should I do next? I want to return the dirt to my grandfather. I try to stuff it back into his mouth. Here you dropped this. There are so many worms. This is very fertile soil. You are so lucky, I tell him. Not everyone lives nitrogen rich. Imagine what kind of gardens could thrive in your mouth. I push more dirt into his mouth. Do you remember the squash that would wind its way around the fence, the pile of reclaimed wood and pipes we saved for some reason or another where a family of cats once lived, then disappeared? My grandfather has a wider mouth than I remember. Which part of my grandfather have I not distorted? I find other things to fill his mouth: sparrow eggs, rosaries made of little plastic meteorites. I have questions: How many uncles did you have? Did you also forget their names? He cannot answer. It starts to snow. He looks beyond me. How did I miss all the disappearing leaves? I have seen his silence before. He forgets what he wanted to say.

SYMPATHY FOR THE CONSPIRACY THEORIST

The world is indeed rotten and inexplicable and who
doesn't wish to see the truth behind the truth? Beyond
the gauzy simulation of public prayers, the latest
promises of chemistry. The problem is, as you see it,
how we come to know. What we find, for example,
on the windowsill are the wasps who entered
through some undiscovered hole of our house,
a thimble of wings I sweep into my palm.
Their carefully wrought mechanisms come
apart between my fingers. What held any of them
together, and what did they do with their suffering?
There must be a reason for this performance
against our glass besides desire, the breeze
on the other side of the window or the fields filled
with photosynthesis and sugar. Let's assume, then,
a hypothesis about wasps that begins here
as a sliver of venom before it is buried
into the brain of another animal, which is
preceded by the atoms that became a poison,
preceded by the engine of stars, preceded by
the ripple in gravity we call prayer. No,
you are right, as you suspect you have always
been. Consider this my apology. There is
always something more to this than this.

ABOUT THE HORSES

The horse has a royal mane.
The horse in a field with dandelions.

I glaze everything with sweat too. Maybe
I could love this horse. Do horses even sweat?

I research this to confirm. More poems
with science. More evidence, please. Meanwhile,

the horse could be my father or my brother.
I don't know yet so I pour enough water

until there is a river the horse must tread
across before a flood arrives. This poem

might be about civilization or America, this poem
might be about the people in my family

who drowned. I need to know more. Focus
on the horse legs churning the water. The horse

has borders—horse divided between hoof and belly,
between tongue and teeth and grass. Tired

of horses, I look elsewhere—the clouds, the cities
of new glass. There's a whole landscape I've ignored

that is full of trees: Which holds an abandoned nest?
Which could carry my grandfather? Instead, I nap

under a tree with its choir of cicadas. I drink Mountain Dew.
I worry this poem has gotten away from me, that now is the time

for restraint. I look up and find my grandfather dangling
his legs off a tree branch. I want this to be a maple tree

but it takes being a birch so I say fine, my grandfather
with his legs hanging from a birch tree. I've never seen

my grandfather with his pants rolled up
to his knees, his veins like roots.

My grandfather the upside-down tree—this should be
the start of the poem, but I leave it here for now

with a promise to move my grandfather towards
the beginning. My grandfather gets impatient, leaves

in the middle of the poem. I try to summon him
back, say this was only temporary, seasonal—I have more

to discuss: his teeth and his hairy chin, the snow
and his eyeballs, his urine and the ocean—how he could

stroll into the woods forever to become
the moon or apple or carpal tunnel

syndrome. He asks
What about the horses?

ADVICE FOR USING BLOOD IN A POEM

If someone suggests you use words besides
blood in your poems, make it part of a recipe

Try dinuguan, for example

Make your blood impossible to avoid

Another name for this dish is chocolate
meat, the name your aunts used to hide
from you the fact you were eating
pork blood with your rice

Other ingredients may include garlic, onions,
liver, pork belly, dried bay leaf,
vinegar, chicken stock, etc.

Say you know the difference between blood and sweetness

Say you hate the taste of liver

Think of the blood in your poem as a lie

Say this is also your blood: the Spanish
explorer Miguel Lopez de Legazpi and the Datu
Sikatuna, who poured blood from their left
arms into the same cup, mixed it
with wine before drinking

Make a sculpture for the promises you have made
with blood that belonged to someone else

Put it on an island you have never visited
and encourage others to see it

Dream about a volcano and an earthquake,
about the gunfire the day they carried
your grandfather to the cemetery after
he cracked his skull on the bathroom floor,
about the hair of your parents sticky
with blood, the glass beneath their skin,
the scabs on their lips

When you came to retrieve
their luggage, their sandy fishing gear
from the wreckage of their car, you found
the bloodstains on the exposed air bags,
the dashboard, the jacket wet
with rainwater wedged between the seats

Consider the insects that gathered around
all the blood you would not touch

Count the number of times
this blood appears

When you close your eyes, what is
the color of your blood?

No cheating

POEM AS MANANANGGAL ALWAYS
LOOKS FOR THE MOON

a fractured poem arrives at night its lower half hidden

on an empty school bus or perhaps a sinkhole

the city ignored despite the petitions you know what

to do next smear garlic or ash around

the waist when split open a poem cannot

be sustained in sunlight go

for a walk eat a spicy hot dog and leave

a trail of salt behind you avoid any tongue

that is hollow but claims to be full poems

that shrivel the belly how does the poem know

where it can be broken you take classes

to answer these exact questions this is why

your family came to America why you forget

the names of your titas the poem asks you

to draw your face   from memory

you start with a map   trace the route

to the center   city of your mouth   *barangay*

the word your mother used   in the margins

of your portrait   the poem leaves

a note in red   of course   the poem

that swallows the lost asks   *how*

do I get here   who is this supposed to be

POEM AS ASWANG WITH TASTING NOTES

desires your liver but waits until you die

when you are sweetest   the polite thing

to do   the poem tells you the earth remains

tender wherever   your body rests

is this the meaning   of sympathy   look up

the word *kapwa*   oh you mean

mother   or sibling   shiny genetics

you mean the family   of poems you buried

take this sheet of paper and rub

your lola's name on it   the poem returns

mouth full of heirlooms   you cannot retrieve

do not reach   if you are not careful

you could wake up a stump   find

a poem chewing   on your cuticles   disregard

the poem that arrives in the rain   wears a newspaper

for a hat   the poem that does not respect

your silence but promises to save you   to show you

more temperate weather   better gas mileage

fresh blacktop for a pickup game   this is not

that kind of poem at all   a poem that dies before it lives

POEM AS KAPRE WHO ROLLS
CIGARS AMONG THE PINES

loiters close   to the moon   close to wires

with hordes of pigeons   the poem carries around

its neck a way   to disappear   You know a poem

by the movement of leaves   you cannot explain by laughter

whose mouth you cannot find   What questions do you ask

when you want a poem to reveal itself?   Careful

as you ascend this poem   Test the limbs that bear

your weight   What do you intend to bring

to its face and the rodents nested under its chin?   A paper

sparrow   A snowball   You come a wish tangled in hair

The city arrives to trim   the trees and roots that split

the sidewalks   a hazard   Ask if the poem can sustain

you now   It will not   One of you must fall

One of you must burn in the mouth

POEM AS ASWANG WHO PASSES CHICKENS FROM ONE MOUTH TO THE NEXT

Before death you part   the poem's lips   push

the tongue aside   no time to be gentle

with your fingers   the poem reveals another poem living

inside of it   how did you miss the small

animals that steer this desire   witness the head

comes first   a poem that fits between

your thumb and forefinger   you are the midwife

now   hold out your hand   a smaller poem falls

into your palm like a plum wet with spit

how does a poem that consumed   this volume of rotten meat
resist

maturation   what happens next   your Catholic education

did not prepare you for this   to swallow a poem

you must choose where   to start

the head or legs   do not bite down

you could unhinge   your jaw   let

the poem slide into your gullet   say Amen

how did you come to this point   a poem cradled

against a navel   tied to a belly with a scarf

it knows when it is ready   to pass

through your skin   you are not the first

to harvest something you did not start   look closely

the poem survives your impatience   nests in the guts

of someone you have not imagined yet

ON THE HISTORY OF THE LINE

On this line, a herd of carabao

On this line, a moon ascends over a volcano

On this line, a flag declares welcome to the empire

All my best lines are stolen from an empire

On this line, a fleet visited and burned the towns closest to the
water

On this line, the smell of hair on fire

This was just the beginning of negotiations

On this line, soldiers uncover a pine box among ruins

They open the pine box and welcome

the small wooden boy inside

On this line, we give the boy a name

Santo Niño

On this line, we give the boy a basilica

On this line, we dip the boy into the river

On this line, the boy lives in a corner of our house

On this line, my brothers and I complain about his thin smile

On this line, we ask the boy to blink for us

On this line, we ask him to forgive us

On this line, the boy visits us before we sleep

On this line, we pray for the unburnt

On this line, we pray for the unexploded devices

The line breaks when my brothers fall asleep, curled on the
    floor like rosaries

The line breaks whenever I eat dairy against my better judgement

The line breaks when I fart in public

The line breaks where a mouse with its head caught in a trap
    refused to die and rattled all morning behind a stove

The line breaks when I collapse the head of the mouse with a
    broom

The line broke when my mother asked me to moisten her dry
    lips in the hospital and I did not know how

It broke when the hospital asked for insurance information and
    I could not provide it

It broke when my mother asked me to shave my father's face,
   and I did not want to cut his skin

It broke when my mother refused my hand because she did
   not need it to cross the ice

It broke when my father fell asleep in the seat next to me as I
   drove home, his jaw shiny and slack

The line breaks if I do not update my Facebook status

The line breaks whenever a picture I post on Instagram only
   receives three likes

The line breaks when whiteness says *I forget you are even Asian
   sometimes*

The line breaks when whiteness says *You are not the kind of
   Asian who just hangs out with other Asians*

The line breaks when whiteness says *I did charity work in the
   Philippines. I probably know more about being Filipino than
   you do*

The line breaks because I got the shits swallowing whiteness

All my lines end in doubt

I leave enough space at the end for prayer

Forgive the line that stains the fingertips

Forgive the line that does not admit what it stole from its parents

Forgive the line that does not clear its browser history

Forgive the line that dissolves before the sentence ends

Forgive the line that fell asleep while FaceTiming

When it does this, I love to watch it breathe

A PILE OF POEMS IS CALLED A NEGATION

One poem on top of another poem.

Another poem stacked on top of that

Like the terrible architecture of a hamburger or an ugly sub.

Until they obscure the clouds.

Until they disrupt the migration of birds.

I call out to the poems at the very top and ask them what they
see.

The poems tell me an ocean on the rise.

They tell me circus elephants, the bald spot on my head.

As if my scalp is a fleshy hole into which my hair disappears.

The poems on the top want to come down.

The poems on the bottom want to climb up.

No, you can't, I say. You live in a delicate ecosystem.

The poems become noisy and sweaty.

They gossip and swear on the dead—

A hive I stare into for too long that makes me dizzy.

I start to think I am a cloud so I walk away.

I get lost walking through a neighborhood

I have never seen.

One house still has its Halloween decorations up:

a bright orange skeleton hangs by the door,

patiently waiting for the leaves to turn gold.

I invite the skeleton to become a poem.

You have so much potential, I promise.

I have made similar promises before, but this time

I do not lie. I am serious.

We could be good together.

We don't have to be better

than this, but we could be.

NOTES

"From the Trees Full of Birdsong Comes Unripe Fruit": The poem is a response to "A Poem as Long as California" by Rick Barot.

"How to Remove a Spike": Annual Good Friday reenactments of the flagellation and crucifixion of Jesus draw hundreds of visitors and tourists to provinces like Pampanga and Bulacan.

"Field Guide for Accidents":

a. The article "The Racial Inequality of Sleep" by Brian Resnick, published in *The Atlantic*, October 27, 2015, was a springboard for many of the ideas in the book and led me to examine research studying the influence race has on sleep.

b. The data for average hours of sleep and sleep quality comes from the journal article "Are Sleep Patterns Influenced by Race/Ethnicity: A Marker Of Relative Advantage Or Disadvantage?" by Dayna A. Johnson, Chandra L. Jackson, Natasha J. Williams, and Carmela Alcántara in *Nature and Science of Sleep* 11 (2019), https://www.ncbi .nlm.nih.gov/pmc/articles/PMC6664254. This study draws its data from the Multi-Ethnic Study of Atherosclerosis (MESA), which observed the sleeping habits of a broad selection of demographics that included people from six different cities who were white, Black, Hispanic/Latinx, and of Chinese descent.

c. In 2017, 91,000 crashes, 50,000 injuries, and 795 deaths were attributed to drowsy driving. The National Highway Traffic Safety Administration lists on its website several suggestions to improve your alertness on the road: https://www.nhtsa.gov/risky-driving /drowsy-driving.

d. The symptoms for sleep deprivation are based on the following article: "The Effects of Sleep Deprivation on Your Body," by

Stephanie Watson and Kristeen Cherney, in *Healthline* (May 15, 2020), https://www.healthline.com/health/sleep-deprivation/effects-on-body.

e.   Information regarding the effect of daylight saving time comes from the following articles: "'Spring Forward' to Daylight Saving Time Brings Surge in Fatal Car Crashes," *ScienceDaily*, January 30, 2020, and "Chronobiological Evaluation of the Acute Effects of Daylight Saving Time on Traffic Accident Risk," by Josef Fritz, Trang VoPham, Kenneth P. Wright, and Céline Vetter, in *Current Biology* 30 (February 24, 2020), DOI: 10.1016/j.cub.2019.12.045.

f.   The line "What did I know, What did I know/of love's austere and lonely offices?" comes from the poem "Those Winter Sundays" by Robert Hayden.

"The Trees Are Motherfuckers": The poem is in response to "On Looking for Models" by Alan Dugan.

"Poem as Manananggal Always Looks for the Moon": The manananggal refers to a creature in Philippine folklore that feeds on the fetus of pregnant women. Manananggal would split themselves in two at the waist. The top half would go fly into the night searching for their prey.

"Poem as Aswang with Tasting Notes": "Aswang" refers to a variety of creatures in Philippine folklore. These creatures often resemble vampires, ghouls, and witches. The poems that appear in section five reference several stories associated with the aswang. One story involves a black baby chicken that an aswang passes from one mouth to the next in order to transfer its power.

"Poem as Kapre Who Rolls Cigars Among the Pines": The kapre is a kind of tree giant that lives in the trees. They are neither good nor bad, but they are known for rolling cigars and mischief.

"On the History of the Line": "Santo Niño refers to the Santo Niño de Cebu, a wooden icon of the Santo Niño that survived the fires set by the conquistador Miguel Lopez de Legazpi.

ACKNOWLEDGMENTS

My deep heartfelt thanks to Mahogany Browne for selecting the book and for the generosity of her words and poems.

Immense gratitude for the extraordinary staff at Beacon Press. A special thank-you to my editor, Nicole-Anne Keyton, for her enthusiasm, insight, and care.

Thank you to the National Endowment for the Arts and the New York Foundation for the Arts, whose support allowed me to complete this collection.

Eternal thanks to the following people for their many kindnesses that helped sustain my writing: Amber Wheeler Bacon, Rosebud Ben-Oni, Sonya Bilocerkowycz, Ralph Black, Maria Brandt, Willa Carroll, Chen Chen, Andrew Ciotola, Christopher Citro, Charlie Cote, Danielle Cote, Kathryn Cowles, Jessica Cuello, Sean Thomas Dougherty, Jonathan Everitt, Noah Falck, Libby Flores, David Forman, Megan Galbraith, John Gallaher, Kristen Gentry, June Gervais, Robert Glick, George Guida, Joe Hall, Rachel Hall, Alicia Hoffman, J. Bailey Hutchinson, Quinn Carver Johnson, Elizabeth Johnston, Keetje Kuipers, Joseph Legaspi, Keith Lesmeister, Tony Leuzzi, Timothy Liu, Lisa Low, Jennifer Maloney, Rebecca Mannery, Peter Mason, Mariana McDonald, Carol McMahon, Phil Memmer, Rena Mosterein, Jae Newman, Danielle Pafunda, Jon Palzer, Michael Prior, Shawna Kay Rodenberg, Luke Rolfes, David Ruekberg, Stan Rubin, Hugh Ryan, Alan Semerdjian, Amy Marie Smith, Erin Elizabeth Smith, Lytton Smith, Michael

Angelo Smith-Torres, Angelique Stevens, David Tilley, Sarah Watkins, Bart White, Jim Whorton, and Mark Wunderlich.

Thank you to my mother and father for their sense of adventure, their courage, and their tenacity.

Thank you, always and forever, to Catie.

Gratitude to these journals for publishing earlier versions of the following poems:

Academy of American Poets Poem-A-Day Series: "Advice for Using Blood in a Poem"

Bear Review: "Remedy"

Bennington Review: "Field Guide for Accidents" (originally titled "Lullaby")

Citron Review: "Punchline"

City Newspaper: "Sympathy for the Conspiracy Theorist"

Connecticut Review: "Poem as Manananggal Always Looks for the Moon"

The Laurel Review: "Outer Banks," "Summer Solstice with Motownphilly as Soundtrack"

Lunch Ticket: "From the Trees Full of Birdsong Comes Unripe Fruit"

Passages North: "About the Horses," "The God I Know Eats with Its Hands"

Pinwheel: "A Colony of Ants Attack My Wrist and I Just Let Them"

Poet Lore: "For All of My Unborrowed and Unspent Joys"

Poetry Northwest: "A Pile of Poems Is Called a Negation," "Mano"

Salt Hill: "The History of Prayer"

South Dakota Review: "You Are Supposed to Cut a Mango into
   Squares," "Flood Warning," and "Every Wilderness Is a
   Province of Teeth"
Triquarterly: "Witness"
Waxwings: "How to Remove a Spike"
West Branch: "On the History of the Line," "Recollection"